STRANGE LAWS AROUND THE WORLD

SIMRAT SACHDEVA

Made with ♥ on the Notion Press Platform
www.notionpress.com

Contents

Contents

Contents

Disclaimer

Although the author have made every effort to ensure that information collected book was correct, the author do not assume and hereby disclaim any liability to any party for any loss, damage, or disruption caused by errors or omissions result from negligence, accident, or any other cause.

- *All the information is based on the internet searches.*

Simrat Sachdeva

ABOUT AUTHOR

Simrat sachdeva is born in Amritsar, Punjab. She has written 'ESSENCE OF LOVE', 'SUSHANT SINGH RAJPUT', 'MY JUMBO BOOK OF POEMS', 'JUSTIN BIEBER', JUDGEMENT OF SUMREME COURT OF INDIA, RHEA CHAKRABORTY VS STATE OF BIHAR', 'AMAZING PLACES OF INDIA'.

For more information you can catch her on Intagram - Simrat_Sachdeva and facebook - Simrat sachdeva.

Contact- Sim.readers@gmail.com

Preface

Every country is different, and every country's laws are different. Sometimes, these laws border on the seriously ridiculous, and other times they point to important cultural values that might be different than your own.

I compiled a list of weird laws around the world you may not believe exist. But when you're traveling, you certainly don't want to wind up behind bars!

CHAPTER I

It's Illegal to Chew Gum in Singapore

Sometimes we all suffer when fools break the rules. After vandals used chewing gum to mess with the Mass Rapid Transit system and the Housing and Development Board spent $150,000 a year to clean gum liter, Singapore banned all gum substances in 1992.

Anyone importing, selling or making gum in Singapore can get fined and/or jail time, with the exception of nicotine and dental gums offering therapeutic value.

Don't get caught blowing bubbles in the streets!

You've probably heard it said that you can get arrested and flogged for chewing gum in Singapore. The truth, as usual, is more complicated than that – but there certainly are strict rules about mastication within the city limits

It is the one thing you can expect foreigners to know about Singapore. Not that it's a tiny island-city that experienced perhaps the greatest economic miracle of all time under the authoritarian stewardship of Lee Kuan Yew, who died on Monday. Not, any more, that the island was the scene of the British Empire's greatest humiliation, when it was conquered by Japan in 1942. No, the thing everybody knows about Singapore is that they'll flog you if you drop your chewing gum. Or that chewing gum is banned. Or something. Basically the country is fastidious as hell.

As usual, the truth is not quite as advertised. Strictly speaking, the possession of chewing gum (and the chewing of it) has never been *illegal in Singapore. What was outlawed, in 1992, was its sale or importation. The trigger, apparently, was the havoc that gum could cause on the country's extremely expensive new underground system – by covering the door sensors, or simply making a mess of the seats. The punishment for illegal gum trafficking was never corporal, but even for a first offence it can include a fine of up to S$100,000 (£49,000) and up to two years in prison. (In 2004, a minor exemption was introduced for "chewing gum with therapeutic value" – deemed to include Wrigley's Orbit – essentially as a favour to the US, in order to close a bilateral trade deal.)*

The effect of the original ban was immediate. Within a few months, chewing gum more or less disappeared from Singapore. Flattened clots vanished from pavements. Train doors went about their business unimpeded. Indeed, this is probably why the ban so resonates with people. For anybody with at least the occasional authoritarian twinge (which is, I'm guessing, all of us), Singapore offers hope that you can "stamp out" even the mildest forms of antisocial behaviour.

Because gum was not the only target. You can indeed be judicially flogged, with a cane, in Singapore, if you are male and under 50. The punishment applies to many crimes, but these potentially include fairly minor matters such as vandalism and – take note – overstaying your visa. If convicted, you will be stripped naked in a prison room, strapped across a frame, and hit across the buttocks several times with a wet rattan cane not exceeding 1.27cm in diameter. (Let us here pause to note that caning was also practised in Singapore, for many years, by the British.)

All pornography is illegal, naturally, including Playboy. In the past, even Cosmopolitan and Sex and the City were banned. It is illegal to drop litter, and to "spit any substance or expel mucus from the nose upon or on to any street or any public place". Penalties for a first offence can be as much as S$2,000, or S$10,000 for doing it three times. In both cases you may also be forced to clean the streets wearing a green vest. Whether because of its laws, or because of its people, Singapore is by all accounts extremely clean.

Penalty for Chewing Gum in Singapore

The Singapore chewing gum penalty is very similar to the littering fines, where you get fined USD 500- USD 1000 on the first offence, and USD 2000 for the repeat offenders.

Many say that the biggest reason behind the progress Singapore has made is the discipline of the people there. To maintain discipline, many such rules have been made.

According to the country's first Prime Minister, Lee Kuan Yew, the biggest obstacle in development could be the indiscipline of the people. Following this, Lee imposed many restrictions across the country.

Why chewing gum was banned in Singapore?

The ban on the sale of chewing gum was initially imposed to reduce gum-related litter in high-rise public-housing apartments, public spaces, and public vehicles.

The gum left in public areas and on lift buttons, mailboxes, and inside keyholes increased the cost of cleaning and sometimes also damaged the equipment.

Apart from this, there is also a heavy fine for leaving gum in public places across the country. In the first instance, a fine of up to Rs 74,000 can be imposed, but in the second case, if caught illegally eating or throwing it in public spaces, a fine of more than Rs 1 lakh and a jail term of 2 years can also be imposed by the authorities.

As far as I know, no one has ever been arrested for chewing gum in Singapore - for the reason that this is not a crime. What is illegal is importing the stuff, and therefore selling it. You can in fact legally even buy gum in Singapore as long as it for "therapeutic" purposes, such as nicotine gum to help people give up smoking. I believe that Customs also turn a blind eye to people bringing in small quantities for their own use

CHAPTER II

Canadian Radio Stations Must Play Canadian Artists

The Canadians are a patriotic bunch. So much so that all Canadian radio stations are required, by law, to play Canadian artists on the airwaves at least 35 percent of the time, especially during the hours of 6 a.m. and 6 p.m., Monday through Friday.

This means that in an hour of radio during the workweek, you'll hear more than 20 minutes of artists like Nickelback, Alanis Morissette,

Celine Dion, Michael Bublé and Justin Bieber — all of whom are proud Canucks.

When a radio station gets its license from the government they have to make a commitment of service that specifies things like how much time they must dedicate to news and sometimes other specific programming. Same thing is basically true in the US. If your local rock radio station has a jazz hour on Sunday nights it's because their license requires a some amount of "alternative" programming.

In Canada this promise of performance includes maintaining a percentage of Canadian content. For Commercial rock stations it's usually 40% between 6AM and 9PM. Some types of stations get lower quotas.

Canadian content is defined using what is called the MAPL system, which stands for Music (composer), Artist, Performance and Lyrics writer, to count as Canadian content a song must have two of these things. So if an American artist records a song with music and lyrics written by a Canadian that counts. Songs recorded in Canada by Canadian artists count regardless of where the music originated. So for example Jennifer Warnes' album Famous Blue Raincoat counts as cancon because it's all songs written by a Canadian.

CHAPTER III

It's Illegal to Run Out of Gas on the German Autobhan

The primary reason for this is, it can be dangerous to try to stop your car on the side of the highway (Autobahn) in an event car has ran out of fuel. This is an human error and can be easily prevented. Most cars give low fuel warning at least 50 kilometers in advance. A simple solution would be to take the nearest exit and refill the car. A person needs to be extremely ignorant to run out of fuel while

driving even when such ample warnings are presented.

With this said, its illegal to run out of fuel on Autobahn and hence is a punishable offence.

CHAPTER IV

It's Illegal to Hike Naked in Switzerland

After Swiss and German travelers decided to make naked hiking a thing in Switzerland a decade ago (really!), Swiss officials reminded folks that a public indecency law still exists and you can be fined if caught in the woods in the buff.

In 2011, a Swiss man was fined more than $100 for his bare-bottomed walk.

A Swiss court has upheld a fine issued to a man for hiking naked past a family picnic in the region of Appenzell, reports the BBC.

The man was fined 100 Swiss Franks ($108) for his naked stroll but appealed the decision since there is no law against public nudity in Switzerland. There is, however, a law against public indecency and this court decision will set a precedent for the whole country: naked hiking is illegal.

However, The Local reports that the court was split over the decision against nude hiking. The publication also published a conflicting report to the BBC saying that the activity is only banned in Appenzell and not in the whole of Switzerland.

CHAPTER V

It's Illegal to Feed Pigeons in Venice, Italy

With thousands of pigeons descending upon Saint Mark's Square and Venice, lured by the the tourists readily handing out food in exchange for Instagram-worthy photos, Venice lawmakers officially made it illegal to feed the pesky fowl in 2008.

It is said the cleanup from the birds cost each citizen €275 per year, so now, the tables are turned. If you're caught feeding the pigeons, you could face fines of up to €700. Better to get the picture-perfect shot of Venice's beautiful bridges instead.

No feeding the pigeons

For more than two decades, Venice has been trying to protect its walls from damage inflicted by pigeons. Back in 1997, the municipality decided to prohibit the feeding of pigeons in order to help maintain the cleanliness of all the surfaces that contribute to the city's splendor with a fine of 500 euros for those breaking the rule. While the original law had treated Piazza San Marco as an exception, pigeons are such a plague on Venice that the ban was extended to include this area in 2008.

They are blamed for spreading dirt and faeces around the city, ruining the valued facades and monuments in the process.

Back in July, thousands of Venetian locals campaigned against the huge numbers of tourists in their city, complaining of the associated rising house prices and convenience shops being replaced for tourist shops.

Other weird foreign laws including a ban on seeing in the ocean in Portugal, although there are no well-known cases of anyone getting caught (unsurprisingly).

CHAPTER VI

It's Illegal to Wear High Heels to the Acropolis

When packing for a trip to Greece, make sure you have the right shoes. The country banned high heels at the Acropolis in 2009, so no stilettos at the Parthenon.

Not sure why anyone would want to make a trek around the ruins and dirt in heels — surely it's tough to walk and will damage the shoes — but the Greeks put this ban in place to protect its ruins from damage caused by the sharp shoes. The ruins are nearly 2,500 years old, so be respectful and wear some soft-soled shoes when you visit.

Authorities put the ban in place in 2009, because sharp-soled shoes add to the wear and tear of national treasures.

"Female visitors must wear shoes that do not wound the monuments," Eleni Korka, Director of Greek Prehistoric and Classical Antiquities, told the Daily Mail in 2009. "These monuments have a skin that suffers and people must realise that."

There are many stylish alternatives

Among the monuments that have experienced wear-and-tear is the Odeon in Athens. Crews last year removed nearly 60 pounds of chewing gum from under the theater's marble seats. Consequently food and high heels are not allowed to the ancient sites. You can always bring water - but dispose of the bottle properly - or chew a gum - but dispose of this in a garbage bin.

CHAPTER VII

Don't Wear Your Winnie the Pooh T-Shirt in Poland

The cuddly little bear all stuffed with fluff also — gasp! — does not wear pants. Because of this, Poland issued a ban on Winnie the Pooh around playgrounds and schools, finding the A.A. Milne character a bit too risqué for the likes of impressionable children.

Best to leave your bear attire at home if visiting this Eastern European country, just to be safe.

Councillors in a small town in Poland have banned Winnie the Pooh claiming the bear is of 'dubious sexuality', is 'inappropriately dressed' and is 'half-naked'.

Officials in Tuszyn, central Poland even attacked author AA Milne, describing him as 'disturbing'.

The town was considering a special mascot for their new children's playground and someone suggested the popular creation.

However, some members of the council attacked the plan, claiming that Winnie the Pooh was a dangerous influence on children.

Councillor Ryszard Cichy, 46, said: 'The problem with that bear is it doesn't have a complete wardrobe.

'It is half-naked which is wholly inappropriate for children.'

He then suggested a Polish fictional bear, saying: 'Ours is dressed from head to toe, unlike Pooh who is only dressed from the waist up.‘

The meeting, which was recorded by one of the councillors and leaked to local press, then turned on Winnie the Pooh's sexuality.

One official is heard saying: 'It doesn't wear underpants because it doesn't have a sex. It's a hermaphrodite.‘

It doesn't wear underpants because it doesn't have a sex. It's a hermaphrodite

Councillor Hanna Jachimska then began criticising the Winnie the Pooh author Alan Alexander Milne.

She said: 'This is very disturbing but can you imagine! The author was over 60 and cut his [Pooh's] testicles off with a razor blade because he had a problem with his identity.'

The councillors have yet to make a formal decision about which bear will be the patron of the children's playground.

But Winnie the Pooh is not a candidate, they said.

CHAPTER VIII

It's Illegal to Ride a Cow While Drunk in Scotland

Before you get any crazy ideas — and have too much Scottish whisky — you should know you could get a ticket for drunk cow riding. Technically, the full 1872 law mandates people not be drunk when in charge of a cow, horse, carriage or steam engine.

In case you are wondering, the same law states you cannot have a loaded firearm on you while drunk. (We have to admit, that's a pretty good rule.)

According to the Licensing Act 1872, it's an offence in Scotland to be drunk while in charge of a cow, horse, carriage or steam engine – or while in the possession of a loaded firearm. If found guilty, according to Scottish Field, you could be jailed for up to 51 weeks.

CHAPTER IX

No Selfies With Buddha in Sri Lanka

When you take a selfie with Buddha, you are turning your back on him. Tsk, tsk. This sign of disrespect is punishable by imprisonment in Sri Lanka. It is also considered disrespectful to point your finger at Buddha, and sometimes there are bans on taking photos with the statues.

Although not illegal to have tattoos of Buddha, a British woman was jailed for three days in 2014 for inappropriate tattoos of the man 70 percent of Sri Lankans feel is a prophet and avatar of the god Vishnu.

Be polite and cover tattoos, respect "no photograph" signs, and don't turn your back on him.

CHAPTER X

It's Illegal to Wear a Mask in Public in Denmark

Not only masks, the Danish government wants to stop anyone from covering their faces in any way in public spaces. This includes masks, helmets, scarves, hats, fake beards and even burkas.

The controversial ban went into effect in August 2018. Officials claim the ban helps to properly identify people during crowded events, should anything negative happen and someone need to be identified.

Government also banned burqa.

"All women should be free to dress as they please and to wear clothing that expresses their identity or beliefs," Gauri van Gulik, Amnesty International's Europe director, said in a statement. "This ban will have a particularly negative impact on Muslim women who choose to wear the niqab or burqa ... The law criminalizes women for their choice of clothing and in so doing flies in the face of those freedoms Denmark purports to uphold."

CHAPTER XI

Registering as Married at a Hotel Makes It So in North Carolina

Let's say a man and a woman walk into a hotel in North Carolina, request to share a room, and claim they are married. By common law marriage rules in the state, that man and woman would legally be married.

As the couple "outwardly present themselves as husband and wife to the public," they are deemed a common law marriage, that is honored and valid in North Carolina.

Should you find yourself in need of a hotel room for the night, you may want to fess up if you aren't a married couple.

CHAPTER XII

It's Illegal to Fly a Kite in Victoria, Australia

In Australia's southeastern tip of Victoria, home to Melbourne, it is illegal to fly a kite in a public space if it bothers another person. In fact, you cannot even play a game in a public place if it annoys someone else.

Listed as part of Summary Offences Act of 1966, the Aussies probably won't mind if you do decide to fly a kite while you visit.

It is an offence to fly a kite "to the annoyance of any person" in a public space in Victoria, with the crime carrying a maximum penalty of $777.30 fine.

CHAPTER XIII

Flying a Kite Is Also Illegal in Buenos Aires, Argentina

Australians aren't the only ones who are apparently opposed to flying a kite. Lawmakers in 1907 Buenos Aires took it a step further by completely stripping the Argentinean capital of the simple joy of flying kites.

In 1989, the law was partially revoked to make it legal to fly kites in squares and parks. But don't even think about trying to enjoy this childhood pastime anywhere else.

The Basant kite flying festival was banned in Pakistan's Punjab province in 2007. The government imposed the ban because of unsafe practices.

CHAPTER XIV

No Water Pistols on New Year's in Cambodia

New Year celebrations in Cambodia get so crazy that the capital city of Siam Reap won't allow for the sale of water pistols leading up to and during its big celebrations. The ban went into place to prevent "traffic accidents" and "public disorder."

Apparently, any other time of year is okay for a water gun fight, but if you go for New Year's, shop owners won't sell you the plastic toy.

CHAPTER XV

It's Illegal to Be Shirtless in Barcelona

In an effort to keep the streets of Barcelona free of beachgoers in bikinis and men going shirtless, lawmakers in the Spanish town on the Mediterranean banned anyone from being topless or in a swimsuit in public anywhere but the beach or a pool.

Passed in 2011, fines for walking around half-naked could cost you up to €260.

No shirt, no shoes, no service!

CHAPTER XVI

It's Illegal to Swear in the U.A.E.

In the Muslim United Arab Emirates, swearing could get you fined, jailed or deported. Under Article 373 of the UAE Penal Code, "swearing disgraces the honour or the modesty of a person."

This isn't just for saying the inappropriate words aloud. It includes indecent physical gestures and extends to your text messages and social media, as well. Not even indecent emojis are allowed.

Earlier this year, the British Express reported a man sent an angry message to a car dealer who seemingly did him wrong. He was threatened with three weeks in jail for his choice of words.

If you have a potty mouth, be sure it's in check before you visit!

CHAPTER XVII

You Cannot Die Without a Pre-Purchased Burial Plot in Part of France

In the town of Sarpourenx, you cannot die within the city limits unless you already have your burial plot purchased in the local cemetery.

This has to do with the fact that the cemetery is full, so the mayor issued an ordinance in 2008. He added, "Offenders will be severely punished."

CHAPTER XVIII

You Must Walk Your Dog Daily in Rome

Rome's strict laws against animal cruelty include the walking of pet dogs. If an owner does not walk their dog once a day (at minimum), they could be fined $625.

The law extends to goldfish as well. While they cannot be walked, they must have room to swim. Goldfish are not allowed to be kept in bowls and must, instead, have a full-sized aquarium.

CHAPTER XIX

You Must Honk When Passing a Car in New Jersey

When driving along the highway in the Garden State, you are legally required to provide an audible warning that you are about to pass a car on the left.

This means that, whether you're driving on the Garden State Parkway or the New Jersey

Turnpike, you technically should honk your horn before you pass, according to state law.

As if the people in Jersey aren't honking enough already.

CHAPTER XX

It's Illegal to Build a Sandcastle in Spain

Spain despises your attempt at making sand castles so much you could be fined if caught building one in Spain.

And the fines vary by location at their discretion. On the island of Majorca, for example, you could pay €100, but you could pay up to €1,500 in Galicia.

Before you ask, yes, kids are included in this restriction — and parents foot the bill.

CHAPTER XXI

Capri May Bust Your Dog With DNA

It's illegal to leave dog waste on the isle of Capri in Italy, as in many places. But for the many dog owners who ignore this law, science is now against you.

If you don't pick up your dog poop, it may be possible to use DNA testing to determine the identity of your dog. And then, you'll be fined.

CHAPTER XXII

It's Illegal to Kill Bigfoot in British Columbia, Canada

When people first began sighting Bigfoot, or Sasquatch, in the 1800s, British Columbia made it illegal to kill him/her/it.

No one has ever captured proof of this hairy, giant creature, but if you should find it and kill it, you could be fined up to $250,000 if you do *not have a proper hunting license.*

Washington State, just below the border, has a similar law.

CHAPTER XXIII

It's Illegal to Wear a Fake Mustache in an Alabama Church

If your fake mustache makes people laugh, save it for anywhere but church, as it is illegal in Alabama. The point of this silly law is that you are not to interrupt the service.So, you can wear a fake mustache to church as long as it doesn't elicit laughter. Just know your audience

CHAPTER XXIV

Married Women Can Only Have One Glass of Wine in Bolivia

If you're a single woman in La Paz, Bolivia, drink up! But if you are married, it's just one glass of wine for you.This sexist law is due to the belief that alcohol may make a woman more immoral. A husband could actually divorce her if she is drinking in public!

CHAPTER XXV

It's Illegal to Disrupt a Wedding in Australia

Even if the preacher asks if anyone has any objection to the wedding, if you are in South Australia, keep it to yourself.

If not, you could be fined up to $10,000 and even spend up to two years in jail if you interrupt a wedding.

CHAPTER XXVI

It's Illegal to Climb a Tree in Toronto

Think you can just climb a tree in Canada? (Why not, there are a lot of them, right?) Expect to pay a hefty fine if you get caught doing so anywhere in the province of Ontario.

This goes for Ottawa, Toronto and even in the middle of the forest — unless you have a permit. In 2013, one young tree-climbing enthusiast earned himself a $365 ticket for climbing one *in Bellevue Square Park.*

CHAPTER XXVII

You Must Provide for Your Elderly Parents in China

The Protection of the Rights and Interests of Elderly People (over the age of 60) includes a number of requirements for children when it comes to their elderly parents.

You may not forsake or insult your parents, you must take care of them.

If not, parents can request alimony!

CHAPTER XXVIII

It's Illegal for Your Chicken to Cross the Road in Georgia

Yep, that's right! In an effort to encourage people to keep their chickens under control, there is a statute in Quitman, Georgia, that says you can be fined if your chicken should get loose.

This means it cannot cross the road to get to the other side.

CHAPTER XXIX

It's Illegal to Pay With Too Many Coins in Canada

When making a payment that is more than $10, it is illegal to pay with more than a single coin under the Currency Act in Canada.

CHAPTER XXX

Close the Gate or You'll Be Fined in Nevada

Gates in Nevada are used to keep in livestock, and anyone not closing and fastening a gate when outside city limits can receive a fine.

CHAPTER XXXI

Don't Pass Wind in Malawi

The "Air Fouling Legislation" of 2011 made it illegal for people in Malawi to "foul the air."

This stirred up a big debate on whether or not this means flatulence is now a criminal offense.

CHAPTER XXXII

It's Illegal to Call a Woman an Unchaste Name in Oklahoma

If any person calls a woman a name that suggests she isn't chaste, whether she is married or single, that person can be found guilty of slander.

A fine of $25 to $500 can be issued if you call a woman a name orally or by other means, so *that means not even cyber bullying should take place in Oklahoma. We can get behind that!*

CHAPTER XXXIII

You Cannot Be Overweight in Japan

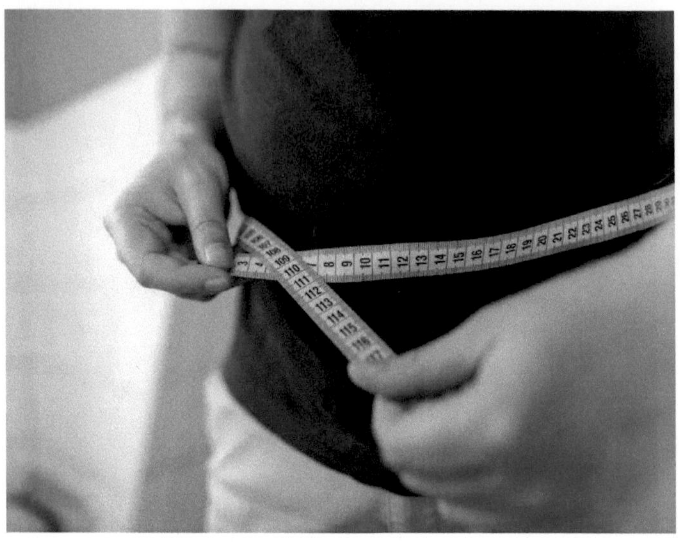

Save for Sumo wrestlers, in an effort to prevent obesity in its citizens, Japan created the Metabo Law. This requires people between the ages of 40 to 74 to have an annual waist measurement performed at the doctor.

Fines will be incurred if men have waists over 33.5 inches or 35.4 inches for women.

CHAPTER XXXIV

Don't Hang Your Dirty Laundry in Public in Trinidad and Tobago

Keep your dirty laundry to yourself in the islands of Trinidad and Tobago, where it is illegal to dry your clothes anywhere that projects over a street, wall, fence or window facing a street.

The islands want to look clean while you're cleaning.

CHAPTER XXXV

It's Illegal to Tell Fortunes in Maryland

Whether it is through tarot cards, palm reading or any other method, fortune telling is banned across the state of Maryland.

If caught, you could receive a fine up to $500 and even up to a year in jail.

CHAPTER XXXVI

You Can't Turn Off Your Phone's Camera Sound in South Korea

As a response to a hidden camera crisis in subways, the South Korean government banned the silencing of phone cameras when taking pictures. This means that if you buy a phone in the country, you will be unable to turn off the shutter sound. This law also exists in Japan.

CHAPTER XXXVII

Finnish Taxi Drivers Must Pay Royalty Fees for Songs They Play in Their Cars

Whenever you get into a cab, it's normal for the taxi driver to be listening to the radio, as a way to make the ride more pleasant for everyone. In Finland, however, taxi drivers are required by law to pay royalty fees for songs they play while driving passengers.

The logic of the law is that they're using the song for business while making a profit, so they must pay for the rights.

We're all for intellectual property protection, but this seems a bit extreme.

CHAPTER XXXVIII

You Can't Flush the Toilet After Hours in Swedenv

If you're in certain parts of Sweden and need to go to the bathroom after 10 p.m., you're out of luck. It's not that you can't go to the bathroom, but you won't be able to make noise while you do it.

This means that you will be forced to let it mellow until the morning. If you're a guy, you'll also need to go sitting down so that you don't make noise.

The rule isn't followed in every part of the country, but if you have an annoying neighbor who wants to complain, they would technically have the law on their side.

CHAPTER XXXIX

It's Illegal to Die Inside the Houses of Parliament

Don't even think about dying inside the Houses of Parliament, or you'll ... actually, we don't really know what the consequences for this crime would be.

Since the building is considered a royal family palace, if anyone dies inside it, they must be buried with full honors. We're not sure how many people were planning to die here, but we guess Britain wanted to be safe.

CHAPTER XL

It's Illegal to Drive a Dirty Car in Russia

Russians care about looks. So much so, that the country has made driving a dirty car illegal here.

Not sure exactly what level of dirt is permitted or how often the rule is actually enforced. But the fact that the law exists — and that it had to have been made within the past 100 years — is fascinating.

Thank you for Purchasing the book

9 798889 512479

Printed by Libri Plureos GmbH in Hamburg,
Germany